Smart About Sports

Meet the Yankees

By
Mike Kennedy
with Mark Stewart

NORWOOD HOUSE PRESS

Norwood House Press, P.O. Box 316598, Chicago, Illinois 60631

For information regarding Norwood House Press,
please visit our website at: www.norwoodhousepress.com or call 866-565-2900.

Photo Credits:
   Getty Images (4, 12, 13, 15, 16, 21), Black Book Partners (7, 23 both), Sportschrome (8, 20), Associated Press (22).
Cover Photos:
   Top Left: The Upper Deck Company; Top Right: Ron Vesely/MLB Photos via Getty Images;
   Bottom Left: Jeff Zelevansky/Getty Images; Bottom Right: Topps, Inc.
The baseball memorabilia photographed for this book is part of the authors' collection:
   Page 6) Alex Rodriguez Card: Topps, Inc.; Page 10) Babe Ruth Card: Kellogg Co.; Joe DiMaggio Card:
   The Upper Deck Company; Yogi Berra Card: Topps, Inc.; Lou Gehrig Magazine: PIC Magazine; Page 11) Mickey Mantle Card:
   Dexter Press; Reggie Jackson Card, Derek Jeter Card, Mariano Rivera Card: Topps, Inc.
Special thanks to Topps, Inc.

Editor: Brian Fitzgerald
Designer: Ron Jaffe
Project Management: Black Book Partners, LLC.
Editorial Production: Jessica McCulloch

LIBRARY OF CONGRESS CATALOGING-IN-PUBLICATION DATA
     Kennedy, Mike (Mike William), 1965-
     Meet the Yankees / by Mike Kennedy with Mark Stewart.
        p. cm. -- (Smart about sports)
     Includes bibliographical references and index.
     Summary: "An introductory look at the New York Yankees baseball team.
   Includes a brief history, facts, photos, records, glossary, and fun
   activities"--Provided by publisher.
     ISBN-13: 978-1-59953-372-8 (library edition : alk. paper)
     ISBN-10: 1-59953-372-3 (library edition : alk. paper)
     1. New York Yankees (Baseball team)--Juvenile literature. I. Stewart,
   Mark, 1960- II. Title.
     GV875.C6K46 2010
     796.357'64097471--dc22

                                    2009043052

Manufactured in the United States of America in North Mankato, Minnesota.
N147—012010

Contents

Words in **bold type** are defined on page 24.

The Yankees celebrate their 2009 championship.

The New York Yankees

New York City has many sports teams. The Yankees are the city's oldest team. They have won the most championships of any team in any sport. Their fans love to watch them play—and win! That is why cheering for the Yankees is a part of family life. And it is why you see children, parents, and grandparents at every Yankees game.

Once Upon a Time

The Yankees played their first season in New York in 1903. They were part of a new league called the American League (AL). The Yankees have always put great players on the field. Their famous hitters include Babe Ruth, Joe DiMaggio, Derek Jeter, and Alex Rodriguez. Their famous pitchers include Lefty Gomez, Whitey Ford, and Mariano Rivera.

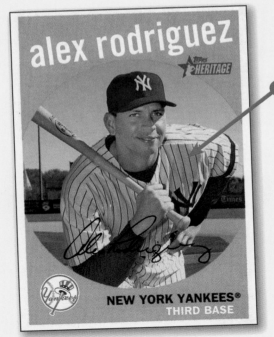

Babe Ruth stands between teammates Bob Meusel and Earle Combs.

Fans fill the new Yankee Stadium for a game in 2009.

At the Ballpark

The Yankees play their home games in Yankee Stadium. It opened in 2009. This new stadium was built across the street from the old Yankee Stadium. They look nearly the same. Left-handed batters love Yankee Stadium. The right field wall is closer to home plate than the left field wall. That makes it easier to hit home runs.

Shoe Box

The cards and magazines on these pages belong to the authors. They show some of the best Yankees ever.

Babe Ruth

Outfielder

- **1920–1934**
Babe Ruth was baseball's first great home run hitter. He was a favorite of boys and girls all over the country.

Joe DiMaggio

Outfielder

- **1936–1951**
Joe DiMaggio was so good that he made baseball look easy. He played in the **All-Star Game** 11 times.

Lou Gehrig

First Baseman

- **1923–1939**
Lou Gehrig played in 2,130 games in a row. A rare illness finally forced him to leave the field.

Yogi Berra

Catcher

- **1946–1963**
Yogi Berra won the World Series more times than any other player. When the Yankees needed a hit, he always seemed to come through.

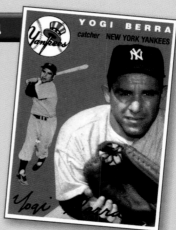

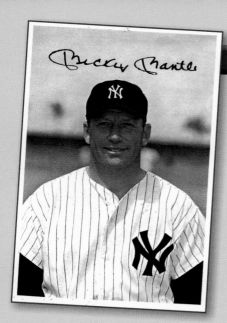

Mickey Mantle

Outfielder • 1951–1968
Mickey Mantle hit long home runs right-handed and left-handed. He won the **Triple Crown** in 1956.

Reggie Jackson

Outfielder • 1977–1981
Reggie Jackson loved hearing the New York fans cheer for him. The bigger the game, the better he played.

DEREK JETER
shortstop NEW YORK YANKEES®

Derek Jeter

Shortstop • 1995—
The Yankees won four championships in Derek Jeter's first six years. He became one of baseball's greatest leaders.

Mariano Rivera

Pitcher • 1995—
Mariano Rivera was the best ever at "closing out" games. When he took the mound in the late innings, hitters had no chance.

MARIANO **Rivera**
N.Y. YANKEES®

ABC's of Baseball

In this picture of Alex Rodriguez, how many things can you find that begin with the letter **H**?

See page 23 for answer.

13

Brain Games

Here is a poem about a famous Yankee:

There once was a pitcher named Ford,
Whose skill just could not be ignored.
When he took the mound,
The hitters would frown.
They knew that few runs would be scored.

Guess which one of these facts is **TRUE**:

● *Whitey Ford won 10 World Series games.*

● *Whitey was Ford's real name.*

See page 23 for answer.

Whitey Ford was one of the best Yankees ever.

The infield crew at Yankee Stadium forms the Y in "Y.M.C.A."

Fun on the Field

Many baseball teams have a mascot.
The Yankees do not. But fans still have
plenty of fun at Yankee Stadium.
The people who work on the field
have fun, too. During the fifth inning,
they work to the beat of the song
"Y.M.C.A." They join the crowd in
spelling out **Y-M-C-A** with their arms.

On the Map

The Yankees call New York City, New York home. The players come from all over the country—and all over the world. Match these World Series Most Valuable Players (MVPs) with the places where they were born:

 1 **Billy Martin • 1952 World Series MVP**
Berkeley, California

 2 **Ralph Terry • 1962 World Series MVP**
Big Cabin, Oklahoma

 3 **Bucky Dent**
• 1978 World Series MVP
Savannah, Georgia

 4 **Mariano Rivera**
• 1999 World Series MVP
Panama City, Panama

 5 **Hideki Matsui**
• 2009 World Series MVP
Kanazawa, Japan

United States Map

The Yankees play in New York City, New York.

World Map

What's in the Locker?

Baseball teams wear different uniforms for home games and away games. New York's home uniform is bright white. It has thin, dark blue stripes called pinstripes. The uniform top has the letters **N-Y**.

Mark Teixeira wears the team's home uniform.

New York's away uniform is gray. The uniform top spells out **N-E-W Y-O-R-K**. The players wear a cap with the letters **N-Y** on the front.

CC Sabathia wears the team's away uniform.

We Won!

The Yankees won their first World Series in 1923. They won their 27th in 2009. Often,

their heroes have been superstars like Lou Gehrig, Mickey Mantle, and Derek Jeter. Other times, players who aren't superstars have led the team. Don Larsen, Bobby Richardson, and Scott Brosius have all been named World Series MVP for the Yankees.

Don Larsen gets a hug from Yogi Berra after an amazing victory during the 1956 World Series.

Record Book

These Yankees stars set amazing team records.

Hitter	Record	Year
Babe Ruth	.393 **Batting Average**	1923
Don Mattingly	238 Hits	1986
Rickey Henderson	93 Stolen Bases	1988

Pitcher	Record	Year
Jack Chesbro	41 Wins	1904
Ron Guidry	248 Strikeouts	1978
Mariano Rivera	53 **Saves**	2004

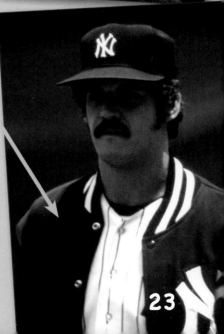

Answer for ABC's of Baseball
*Here are words in the picture that start with **H**:*
Hand, Heel, Helmet, Hip.
Did you find any others?

Answer for Brain Games
The first fact is true. Whitey Ford pitched 16 seasons for the Yankees and went 10–8 in the World Series. His real name is Edward Charles.

Baseball Words

ALL-STAR GAME
The game played each season between the best players from each league.

BATTING AVERAGE
A measure of how often a batter gets a hit. A .300 average is very good.

SAVES
A number that shows how many times a pitcher comes into a game and completes a win for his team.

TRIPLE CROWN
An honor given to a player who leads the league in home runs, batting average, and runs batted in.

Index

Photos are on **bold** numbered pages.

About the Yankees

Learn more about the Yankees at newyork.yankees.mlb.com

Learn more about baseball at www.baseballhalloffame.org